NEXT DOOR,
DOWN THE ROAD,
AROUND THE CORNER

NEXT DOOR, DOWN THE ROAD, AROUND THE CORNER

A Family Album

RICHARD BALZER

DOUBLEDAY & COMPANY, INC.
GARDEN CITY, NEW YORK
1973

DESIGNED BY EARL TIDWELL

ISBN: 0-385-05345-2 Trade
       0-385-05407-6 Paper
Library of Congress Catalog Card Number 73-76449

To Eileen, my QB

Acknowledgments

It is very difficult to think of something to say to the people I feel most in debt to. All I can say is that I hope my gratitude is enough of a thank you to the endless number of people who let me share part of their lives. I hope this book will accurately reflect some of the realities of those lives.

Each time I started one of my trips I had a pile of names. Of all the friends who recommended people to see, I want to take this opportunity to thank three, Paul Ylvisaker, Wilton Dillon, and Taylor Branch, because without the names and references each gave I would have seen much less than I did.

Once I was on the road new adventures always opened up. One that I will remember fondly is the five days I spent with the gospel-singing Oak Ridge Boys, riding around Tennessee, Kentucky, and Georgia. I really enjoyed myself and wished I had the time to go with them on their California tour.

During my first trip to the West Coast I discovered that without a press card I would miss a lot of things. I traveled without one for several months until I met Michael Howard, editor of the *Rocky Mountain News*. I appreciate Michael's giving me press credentials, for it helped a lot.

I want to thank Shep Shepherd, Larry Saliameno, and David and Ronnie Deutsch, without whose special help I couldn't ever have finished this book.

Away from my own darkroom I was always looking for someone else's to use. Several people helped in this regard but no one was more generous with his time and equipment than Ray Komorski, who repeatedly let me use his studio. His Chicago studio became my Midwestern base, and his assistant, Windy Greavner, time and again helped me with my work.

I also want to thank Elsa van Bergen and all the other people at Doubleday who had faith in this project.

I need to thank John Hill, who with his usual endless patience spent countless hours going over my material. He showed me that a book, like a tree, can stand a good pruning.

Last of all to my wife, to whom this book is dedicated, I want to say I love you. ■

These are really the thoughts of all men in all ages and lands, they are
    not original with me,
If they are not yours as much as mine they are nothing, or next to nothing,
If they are not the riddle and the untying of the riddle they are nothing,
If they are not just as close as they are distant they are nothing.
This is the grass that grows wherever the land is and the water is,
This is the common air that bathes the globe.

WALT WHITMAN
Leaves of Grass

Once when I was twelve my parents took the family cross-country on a Santa Fe Railway tour. I can still recall the entire trip. I remember the film of frost my nose and lips left on the large plate glass windows as I strained to get a better view of the passing countryside. I remember the dome car in which I sat and looked at the starlit sky, an astronomy book on my lap to identify Leo, the Dippers, and Pisces. I remember the wonderful special feeling of eating and sleeping on a moving train. I remember stopping at the Grand Canyon, Las Vegas, and Disneyland.

Ever since, I have loved this country, contemplated its size and how I would explore it someday. A few times I actually got started, but it was never long enough, never far enough. Over the years my desire to see the country has not diminished. It has changed as I have and has grown in intensity.

After four years of college and three years of law school I decided it was time for me to explore America before my trip became a wistful daydream. Once the decision was made the first thing I did was look for a car I could travel and live in.

For two days a friend and I looked through Chicago's used-car lots. We examined old vans, air-conditioned vans, and vans that wouldn't start, before finding a 1967 Ford Econoline.

Outfitting the van took the better part of a busy day. With an old rug and foam padding the van's metal floor was transformed into sleeping quarters. My wife, Eileen, made curtains, while I stocked up on utensils, a portable stove, and canned food. Eileen, who doesn't like me to eat like a slob, added paper towels, napkins, and a lot of little things that I would probably never use: a deck of cards, an extra bottle opener, two small note pads, and a corkscrew.

The van held a few other items: books to read, a paper to finish, and a thirty-year-old Remington Rand typewriter which never quite made up its mind whether it preferred to skip extra space or have none at all between words. A Hadassah thrift shop suitcase held my clothes.

By this time the van was pretty full, but I took a few extra items. A friend gave me a strand of Indian prayer beads which he promised would keep evildoers away. A couple from Japan sent me a traveler's kit: wooden flute, compass, and small sewing set. Almost as soon as I began my trip I picked up a toy racing car, which a boy in a trailer camp traded me for a kite I had. The little blue car with its red driver has rested on my dashboard ever since. The last thing I collected was a souvenir coin at Governor George Wallace's inauguration. There is a likeness of Wallace on the front and an eagle on the back. The coin is inscribed, "Let the people speak, stand up for America."

In eighteen months I traveled more than 50,000 miles in the van. It took two flat tires on the same wheel before I got tired of riding on treadless rubber and bought a pair of new tires. It was a good four months and two more flats before I changed the other tires. Hard driving plus wear and tear took their toll: I lost the packing in a wheel bearing one Sunday, near Missoula, Montana. The accelerator cable froze and broke, the emergency brake wore out, and the heater stopped working. The van seemed to dislike snow, so I avoided it whenever possible. Nevertheless, I occasionally found myself on the shoulder of a road.

My greatest concern was not about the van or my equipment but about myself. Before I began traveling I made myself one promise: I would not tell a lie. This may not sound like much of a promise, but I thought it might prove to be difficult, as I hoped to spend considerable time with people with whom I might violently disagree, and be in situations from which my activities and appearance had previously excluded me. What would happen when a discussion became heated and someone wanted to know my views? Could I, or for that matter should I, keep my mouth shut?

Once I had decided that I wanted to observe people and not judge them, I realized that the best thing I could do was be quiet, try to listen. I was surprised at how infrequently I was even put to a test. Almost no one ever pushed me to express an opinion. Sometimes I did feel that I wanted to vent my outrage—scream out, beat my chest, express moral indignation—but I didn't. Once or twice I left a place after listening too long, feeling saturated with hatred.

One of the first things I learned on the road was that to be a good observer one has to be inconspicuous. Some of this is not very difficult. I wear plain clothes, and try to make the fact that I am carrying cameras as unnoticeable as possible. There is no good way to hide cameras, but one certainly doesn't need to wear them draped around the neck as an advertisement. I carried my two Nikons, which were stolen from my Philadelphia apartment less than two months after I completed my traveling, in a plain black leather bag.

I realized that my hair and mustache would exclude me from some situations, would make many people hostile or suspicious, so before going to the South and the Southwest, I shaved off my mustache and trimmed my hair. Both times I was pleased that I had done the right thing. Shorn of my locks, I traveled less noticed, was more able to gain entry to a wider range of situations. However, to my surprise, many long-haired youths—whom I had always regarded as my peers—now viewed me with suspicion and occasionally some hostility. My short hair opened many doors, but it closed a few as well.

Despite this effect I returned each time determined to keep the mustache off and my hair short till I finished my work. When I would tell my wife, she would protest, saying that the hair could stay short but that she liked my face better with the mustache. My mother-in-law, in an unguarded moment, said that the mustache hid some of my nose. In this matter I bent to my family's opinion.

I saw the country not in one long trip, but in several trips that ranged from four days to six weeks. My first trip took me through northern California into the Pacific Northwest and across the northern mountain states. I had made all sorts of plans: what to do, where to go, what to accomplish.

After a few days on the road I found that I was often moody, even irritable. It was, I discovered, because I was making impossible demands on my trip. Each day had to produce something, a special picture or a good story, no matter what the weather, the circumstances, or my mood. It took me time to learn that a trip has its own logic, and that I could not force a day to respond to my needs or time schedule. I had to accept the long, seemingly unproductive hours and days. They were as much a part of the trip as the crowded, busy days. I had to teach myself to be less anxious, and to try to relax and watch for opportunities.

Each trip thereafter began in the same way. I would pick a part of the country that I wanted to see, a good season in which to visit it, and a general route to follow. I would then begin collecting names of people to contact. By the time I left I not only would have a pile of names and addresses, but also lists of places I couldn't miss and things I ought to do.

I was always anxious to start a trip; excited, and full of energy, although nervous and afraid of missing something. Because of this I tried on the first day of each trip to find an artificial focus, an event of some sort, where I could overshoot and ease my tensions. After a few days I would begin to relax and settle into the trip. As each trip unfolded I relied less and less on the names I had and began to explore more, staying with people I met on the road or in a quiet state park or roadside rest where I could be alone.

Throughout my travels I encountered a tremendous kindness, an openness and warmth shown a stranger which I believe is peculiar to Americans. I arrived in Ellensburg, Washington, a day before a big rodeo, and feeling lazy I found a shady stoop along Main Street from which to view the local traffic. I must have been sitting there for over an hour when someone asked, "Hey, didn't I meet you at the rock festival outside of Portland?"

I looked up at the girl who had just spoken to me, but I couldn't place her until she started humming a tune. Then I remembered the dusty gray dancing area and the girl who had hummed the tune. We talked for a while and I ended up staying at her boy friend's apartment. I stayed that night and the next. On the morning of the third day they left for Seattle, leaving me alone in the apartment. I stayed one more night, locked up, and left.

This incident was the first of many generous gestures. Within a week I met a young architect in Montana, and when I saw him again in Boston in the fall, he gave me the keys to his cabin in Maine. A state legislator with whom I talked for twenty minutes in Montgomery, Alabama, made a house available to my wife and myself in Mobile during Mardi gras. In Houston I took a picture of two couples picnicking, ten-gallon hats, boots, western shirts and all. Before I knew it I was joining them for a fried chicken, chocolate chip cookie Sunday dinner.

It wasn't the last I would see of free chicken meals. Mrs. Mary Lou Smith, of Alpine, Texas, even gave me her recipe for BBQ sauce, to, as she said, carry home to my wife.

¼ cup oleo	1 teaspoon Worcestershire sauce
2 teaspoons catsup	1 teaspoon salt
2 teaspoons lemon juice	1 teaspoon pepper
2 teaspoons vinegar	2 teaspoons horseradish

Melt the oleo, add the other ingredients. Brush on chicken or beef.

There was always someone in a bar who was willing to buy me a drink. Time and again strangers allowed me to sleep on a couch or a spare bed. People whom I met would feed me, invite me into their homes, send me off with a sandwich.

Hitchhikers played an important part in my travels. For someone who drives long distances there are all sorts of practical reasons to pick up hitchhikers, especially hitchhikers who are willing to drive. I found that just to be relieved at the wheel for an hour or two, to close my eyes and relax or catch a quick nap in the back, made a long trip much shorter.

Occasionally there would be a rider with nothing to say, someone who just wanted to ride without conversation. I suppose I had no right to expect more, but each time this happened I felt cheated. Most of the time, though, riders were willing, often anxious, to talk and do some driving. Occasionally they had some money for gas or a snack, and some even led me into unexpected adventures. People had filled my ears with sordid stories about the victims of hitchhikers, but I found the people who travel the roads to be very decent, and to have interesting stories about their own lives and the places they have been. There are many riders I remember.

There was an old retired soldier who smelled of wine and musty clothing. He was going from Kansas City to St. Louis to get some teeth pulled for free at a dental school. He was familiar with the road and talked about places he had gone and seen since the Thirties, how it was harder to ride the rails now than it used to be, and how he stuck to the roads because of that. He was a man who knew a lot, including the locations and requirements of all the Salvation Army Harbor Light Inns between Kansas City and Chicago.

Then there was a young guy with hair down to his shoulders, droopy beagle dog eyes, and a big handlebar mustache. He didn't stop talking from the minute he got in the van till I left him off. He was heading east from California. Before he had started his trip, he had thought he would take a job in New York; now he just wanted to get out of the country.

"Listen, man," he said, "I can't take it any more. People in this country have lost their senses. In the last two weeks I've been thrown

12

in the pokey in Nevada for hitching and had the shit kicked out of me by a group of short-haired creeps in Salt Lake City. I'm telling you, people have gone mad. I'm leaving before it happens to me. It's quite a thing when you don't feel safe in your own country."

And there was the pink-cheeked boy I picked up in Montana. He was about to begin college, and he told me how he worried about school. It was going to be his first time away from home, and he was afraid the more experienced kids would find him too square with his short hair and small-town ways. We talked about it for a long time—college, tests, marijuana, girls—before we got to Bismarck, North Dakota, where he lived. For most of the trip Jerry had called me *sir*. Now, his chest all puffed up, he turned and said, "Listen, Dick, before you let me off, how about letting me buy you dinner?"

"Thanks, Jerry, but I got a can of beef in the back and I'll just cook it up."

"Please," he said, "let me buy you dinner. I want to."

We drove past several restaurants before settling on a $1.49 steak house where we had a good meal. After dinner he headed for home and I got back on the highway going east.

Just as a trip begins, it must end. The ending cannot be planned, at best it can be approximated. No matter how short the trip I took, I found that after a point, never the same point, I became restless with the journey, tired of observing. All of a sudden I would become emotionally exhausted, tired of meeting new people no matter how kind they were. I always missed my wife, but as a trip stretched out I would begin to miss my friends and all the familiar surroundings that make a home something special. Whenever the end of a trip was apparent I headed for home as quickly as I could, never dawdling, never changing my mind. Twice I drove more than 800 miles without stopping in order to get home.

It never ceased to surprise me that after every trip I would inevitably be asked, Well, what's America like? What are people thinking about? What does such and such a group think about this or that?

I have never believed that one worker's response was the working-man's view, nor that one student could tell anyone what students want. I didn't try to collect all the different conversations I had and compile them into a theory. I approached people not to find out what they thought of the issues of the day, but to share in something of their lives, to document what I could.

When I began my trip in Chicago on a hot June day, I didn't know what I would find. There were evenings in New Mexico with more stars than a person who grows up in the East ever gets to see. There was the chilling quiet of a hidden lake. There were rodeos, state fairs, ball games, factories, communes, rural people, small-town folks, and city people. There were machines, buildings, country, and roads. I fell in love with America again, but this time with the people. This is a story about these people, who they are and how they live. ■

ROUTE 94, NORTH DAKOTA

OAKLAND, CALIFORNIA

PHILADELPHIA, PENNSYLVANIA

ALEXANDRIA, LOUISIANA

17

HOLDENVILLE, OKLAHOMA

BOSTON, MASSACHUSETTS

18

PORTLAND, OREGON

NEW YORK CITY

TAOS, NEW MEXICO

NEW YORK CITY

CHEVY CHASE, MARYLAND

HOUSTON, TEXAS

DALLAS, TEXAS

CHICAGO, ILLINOIS

EVANSTON, ILLINOIS

24

EVANSTON, ILLINOIS

WASHINGTON, D.C.

Each year Washington's crowded social calendar includes the Washington Symphony Ball. A lot of time and effort go into making the ball a financial and social success. Three months before the ball I went to a meeting at the home of a planning committee member. There was no one at the door to greet me, so after ringing the bell I walked over a series of small Persian rugs, and then down a flight of well-polished wooden stairs into the large living room, which was already full of neatly dressed women chatting with one another.

Before long the hostess and the committee's secretary moved to a table at the front of the room. The rest of the women moved to chairs and couches scattered around on the parquet floor.

The black gavel hit the table and the meeting was called to order. The first order of business was the reading of last month's minutes. The secretary's report was followed by reports from a number of committee chairwomen about party favors, invitations, and programs. This year's ball

27

would be done in Italian motif, suggesting the great Italian contribution to opera. Even the menus would be printed in Italian.

One of the women on the decorations committee reported on her selection of tablecloths. She had brought some samples with her which she passed around while she continued talking. She suggested that rather than have all the tablecloths one color, they could be different colors with the same pattern. Not only would it be attractive, but the tablecloths could, she said, be sold along with the centerpieces after the ball, for additional revenues.

Everyone agreed that that was a splendid idea. One woman brought a note of caution to the discussion when she said, "Ladies, I agree that selling items after the ball is a good idea, but we will have to be very careful about storing the things so they aren't stolen."

"Yes," said another woman, "it is a problem. You won't believe it, but last year people actually broke into a storage room at the Sheraton and stole things."

Everyone agreed that precautions were necessary, and the problem of security was left in the hands of the woman in charge of tablecloths, to be discussed with the hotel manager.

The longest discussion of the morning concerned dress and the invitation. The chairwoman began by saying that dress for the ball was causing some problem. They weren't quite sure what to do. They had discussed it with the very helpful people at the Italian embassy, and the Italian ambassador had expressed a preference for white tie. However, the chairwoman continued, she was aware of the fact that many people didn't like the idea, and much preferred black tie. Because of this she was wondering what the group thought of having the invitation say either *white tie optional* or *white tie if convenient*.

The first few women who spoke on the matter spoke in opposition to white tie. One said she thought white tie was simply too formal. Several women nodded their heads in agreement. Others expressed more immediate and personal opposition, saying either that their husbands didn't own a white tie and it seemed like a wasteful added expense on top of the $100 ticket price, or that their husbands didn't like wearing white tie. One woman even said, "If it's white tie, I know my husband won't come."

Several women spoke in favor of white tie. A few mentioned the fact that the Italian ambassador seemed keen on it, and that the committee should go along. Others felt that the ball was to be exquisite, and that white tie was very appropriate and tasteful. One woman said that the men wearing white tie would make the ball that much more special and memorable.

Just as the conversation seemed to be getting nowhere, several women began attacking the idea of white tie in regard to the invitation. "Certainly," said one woman, "we can all agree that an informal invitation with *white tie* at the bottom would be in poor taste."

Just then the woman in charge of invitations asked the chairwoman for permission to speak. She said that she was sorry that she didn't have an actual invitation there to show them, but that it wasn't really an informal invitation. Maybe she had given them the wrong impression. If so she was sorry. The invitation would actually be fairly formal, the only real change from last year's being the jagged edge instead of the traditional straight edge.

The chairwoman once again suggested that possibly *white tie optional* or *white tie if convenient* might prove to be a good compromise. Here, though, the women appeared to agree. Almost no one was in favor of the option. The comments ranged from the inappropriateness of such a choice to the remark that those who don't want to come in white tie simply won't, so there is no reason to make an option. One woman concluded the remarks by saying, "It's sad, don't you think, when a room is half black tie, half white tie?" It was agreed that there should be no option, that the choice was either white tie or black tie.

The argument about white tie-black tie began to repeat itself. Sensing the repetition, the chairwoman called on two women who had been quiet during the entire discussion. The women did not agree: the first came out in favor of white tie, the second in favor of black tie.

The chairwoman finally put the question to the women for a vote. The vote was a 12–12 tie. "Ladies, because of the vote," the chairwoman said, "I will appoint a subcommittee of three to make the decision after consultation with the Italian ambassador."

There were a few more committee reports, and they led to a discussion of entertainment. There was general agreement that since people were spending a lot of money there should be good, lighthearted entertainment. The chairwoman said that she had heard only last week that at a White House dinner the table with Secretary Connally had been held in laughter all night by the remarks of a Joe Garagiola. She continued, "Many of my friends say he's a very funny man, and I thought we might ask him to be M.C." The idea met with approval. "All right, ladies, then I'll write Mr. Garagiola and ask him to be M.C."

"I also thought we might use a singer, and I was wondering what you thought about the Italian singer Emberdingle Humberdingler." The remark was met by giggles. Finally a woman said, "No, no, Claire, his name is Engelbert Humperdinck."

Another woman said, "Yes, Claire, and he's English, not Italian."

Emberdingle Humberdingler was put aside and discussion turned to the program, which was to be sold after the ball as a calendar. The committee had tried to get companies or wealthy individuals to sponsor a page. For the fifty-two weeks they had tried to get fifty-two sponsors, each sponsor paying $1,000 for the privilege of his or her name appearing at the bottom of a page. I mentioned to the woman next to me that they must bring in a lot if they charge that kind of money plus $100 per ticket for the ball. She remarked that last year they made more than $100,000 for the Symphony.

Soon after this exchange the meeting ended. The women retired to another room for sherry, liver pâté, and conversation. ■

WETUMPKA, ALABAMA

ROUTE 377, TEXAS

COLUMBUS, INDIANA

PHILADELPHIA, PENNSYLVANIA

WASHINGTON, D.C.

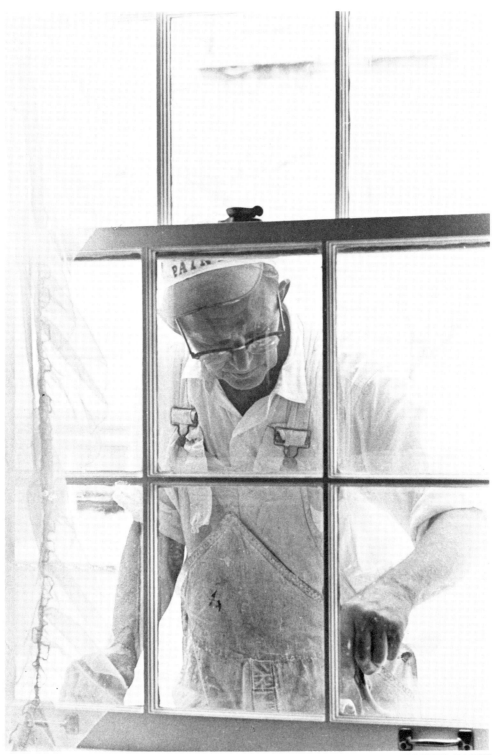

EVANSTON, ILLINOIS

BETHLEHEM, PENNSYLVANIA

CLEVELAND, OHIO

36

ANDOVER, MAINE

TALLAHASSEE, FLORIDA

37

GREAT FALLS, MONTANA

COLUMBUS, INDIANA

INDIANAPOLIS, INDIANA

PROVIDENCE, RHODE ISLAND

CLEVELAND, OHIO

41

It was late afternoon when I picked up barefooted, fishing pole-carrying Reggie and Gregg Stone.

"Where you going?" I asked.

"Down the road a spell," Reggie answered. "Going fishing."

"The fishing any good?" I asked.

"Ain't bad for a little pond,"said Reggie. "Wanna come?"

"Huh, yeah, I would."

We drove in silence until Gregg said, "You know, mister, I sure would like to drive this thing."

"Come on," I said, "you can't drive a car."

"Yup, he can," said Reggie. "Gregg's a good driver and he can drive just about anything."

"Is that right, Gregg? Where did you learn to drive?"

"Taught myself," he proudly said. "Wrecked part of a truck once but now I can drive just about anything."

Reggie tugged on my shoulder, and pointing to a clump of trees just ahead told me to stop. I pulled off the road onto the grass and Gregg swung the door open and jumped out, stopping only long enough for Reggie to throw him his fishing rod before he ran and slid down the embankment to the pond's edge. Reggie was right after him and I followed.

Reggie and Gregg sat a few feet from the pond's edge, sorting through the weights, hooks, and bait in their gear box. Each of them rolled up a small piece of bread, spit on it, and put it on his hook.

I asked Gregg, "Why do you spit on the bait?"

Swinging his line into the water, he said, "Good luck."

Almost as soon as Reggie cast his line in the water he pulled up a fish. He had a big grin on his face as he took the hook out of the fish's mouth. Squeezing the still-squirming fish he showed it to me. Gregg looked at it and said, "Throw it back, Reggie, it's too small."

But Reggie put it by his feet and, spitting on another piece of bread, baited his hook again. For nearly an hour, the sky full of dusky oranges and reds, we sat by the bank. Reggie and Gregg pulled in an occasional small fish and I rested in the shade of a large dogwood tree.

After a while Reggie asked me if I wanted to do a little fishing.

"Sure," I said, and Reggie disappeared to the other side of the pond where he had hidden another rod and reel for emergencies. While he was gone I asked Gregg how old he and Reggie were.

"Reggie is fourteen and I'm almost twelve."

"Does your father mind your fishing this late?"

"Heck no," Gregg said, "he doesn't mind at all."

"What's your father do?"

"My father's dead," said Gregg.

Just as I was struggling to find something appropriate to say, Reggie returned with the extra fishing pole. Gregg took it from him and baited it for me, remembering to spit on the bread. I had no luck my first two casts. Then on my third cast Reggie yelled, "Yank," and I yanked and pulled up a fish.

Reggie and Gregg were getting restless. They had given up on the rolled bread and switched to bugs, coated with flour. Reggie told me the fishing wasn't any good here today. He and Gregg were fixing to go up to the lake for a night of fishing. He asked me if I wanted to come along.

I told him I had to be in Midwest City by eight-thirty the next morning and I would think about it. Our luck didn't change and finally I said, "OK, let's go up to the lake."

Reggie and Gregg looked at each other, smiled, and started packing up all their gear. The lake was a good 10 miles away, and on the way we stopped for a pizza. There was a scroungy dog on the side of the restaurant, sniffing around the garbage cans. Reggie pulled out one of the two tiny fish we had kept for bait and threw it to him. We went inside and ordered a large pizza with everything on it. It took about twenty minutes for it to come and about four minutes for us to polish it off.

During dinner Reggie said he could cook better pizza.

"Cook a lot at home?" I asked.

"Yup, cook all the time. I like cooking fish best."

Gregg licked the borders of his lips with his tongue and said, "Reggie can cook some catfish real good."

Reggie turned to me a toothy grin and said, "You'll see, we'll catch some fish tonight and I'll cook breakfast for the three of us."

Before we left I asked Reggie if they should call their mother and tell her where they were going. He told me she knew; they did this sort of thing often and she didn't mind.

It was pitch-dark when we got to the lake. Reggie and Gregg hopped out of the van and set up the poles again. Then they both took off around a bend to fetch some firewood. After a while they returned, Reggie's arms piled high with wood and Gregg's full of newspapers.

Reggie took care of making the fire while Gregg and I put our poles in the water. We couldn't have been sitting there for more than ten minutes before it began raining. It drizzled for a while and we ignored it. Then the thunder and lightning began and it started pouring. Gregg and I dashed to the van. Reggie stayed outside trying to move his now-smoking fire under cover. By the time Reggie gave up on the fire and came inside he was soaked. We decided to forget about the fishing for the night and get some sleep.

With the rain beating down on the roof, Reggie and I folded up in the back. Gregg took a blanket and crawled into the driver's seat, where he said he was planning to sleep. Just as I was falling asleep I heard Gregg turn on the radio and looked up to see him sitting in the driver's seat, both hands wrapped around the steering wheel. ■

OKLAHOMA

44

BAILEY ISLAND, MAINE

EUREKA, PENNSYLVANIA

NEW HAMPSHIRE

48

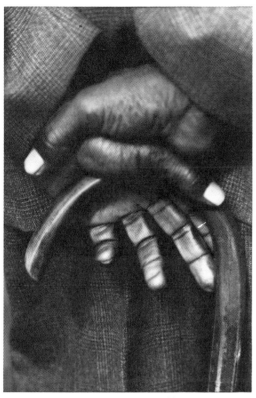

LUMPKIN, GEORGIA

BENEVOLENCE, GEORGIA

WRIGLEY FIELD, CHICAGO, ILLINOIS

The man in charge of press credentials at the 1971 All-Star Game took my *Rocky Mountain News* press card, studied it for a minute, and then asked me how So-and-So was.

"Oh, he's fine," I said, trying not to pause or show that the only person I knew on the *Rocky Mountain News* was the editor who gave me a press pass as a favor. I stood there hoping he wouldn't ask me anything more about the paper or Denver. Luckily, he just jotted my name down on a pass and said, "You'll be seated in a cage over third base. Sorry I can't give you a clubhouse pass, there aren't any left."

I was glad to get out of the room with my press pass, an All-Star Game lapel pin in red, white, and blue, and passes for a sportswriter's lunch and dinner. Only one more thing to do: pick up a name tag. There wasn't much of a line in the lobby, just another guy and me. The woman behind the desk asked the other guy his name.

"Leonard Koppett," he said.

"And what paper are you with, Mr. Koppett?"

Before I knew quite what I was doing I was saying, "What paper is he *with?* He writes for the *New York Times.*"

I couldn't help myself; the words came rushing out before I could control them. I wanted to take them back, but couldn't, so stood there with a silly look on my face.

The woman immediately apologized, saying, "I'm sorry, Mr. Koppett, I should have recognized you, and certainly should have known what paper you write for."

He assured her for the next five minutes that it was perfectly reasonable that she didn't know who he was or for whom he worked. I stood there the whole time, straining to be a tree.

I escaped from the lobby to the press room just in time to catch a part of a press conference with Vida Blue, the year's pitching sensation. I arrived as reporters from all over the room were shouting their questions.

"Vida, is it true you carry two lucky dimes?"

"Yes."

"Where do you carry them?"

"In my back pocket."

"If you win twenty games will you get a third coin?"

"No, I think I'll stay with the same two coins."

"Do you still have the two original dimes?"

"Yes."

"Isn't it true," another voice from the back of the room shouted, "that you lost them in Baltimore?"

"No. I mislaid them. Someone went to make a long-distance call and borrowed them, but I got them back."

"Is there any way you can identify these two particular coins?"

"Yes. Both of them have 'In God We Trust' printed on the back."

Several reporters had hospitality bags under their arms. I asked where they were being given out, and then went back upstairs to fetch my goodies. Just as I was about to enter the room where the bags were, a big old man bellowed in a most unfriendly way, "Where do you think you're going?"

"Inside to get my gift."

"Who are you?" he asked in an equally gruff voice.

"Dick Balzer," I timidly answered, "with *The Rocky Mountain News.*"

"Where's your press credentials?"

I showed him the pass I had gotten upstairs.

"Not that," he said, "your press card."

I fished in my wallet and found my card again. He looked it over, and with some hesitation got me a hospitality bag. I had put myself through all that for the following gifts:

1. a commemorative coin from Cadillac.
2. three different model cars.
3. a pen with a bank's name.
4. an Oldsmobile deck of cards.
5. the American Constitution, including the first ten amendments, from Freedom Foundations.
6. a penny key chain from a bank.
7. a little phone book.
8. a Ballantine Scotch note pad.
9. a Harvey Wallbanger tee shirt.
10. a kazoo.

That was it till the evening party for newspapermen. After dinner I ended up sitting at the New York sportswriters' table. Within minutes I realized that not only was Koppett there, but Red Smith and Dick Young were there too. I mean, *Dick Young.* I used to buy the *New York Daily News* just for the pictures and Young's sports column. Other New York writers, whom I didn't know, were there, all of them busy talking about players and teams, about what was happening to the Mets, and what Tom Seaver's pitching problems were.

The conversation moved to the signing of bonus babies when Al Campinalos, general manager and former chief scout of the Los Angeles Dodgers, sat down. When you're trying to sign a kid, he said, the most important thing is to figure out which parent makes the family decisions and work on that parent. You can't judge by who talks the most; some women don't say very much but they end up making the decision. You have to pay attention all the time, look for little signals. "Generally," Campinalos added, "we've found that the fathers are interested in the money you're offering, and the mothers in their son's welfare with the club."

But there was only so much serious talk allowed. Suddenly, everyone was telling Yogi Berra stories. One story had it that Berra walked into Toots Shor's while Shor was having drinks with Ernest Hemingway. Shor introduced Berra and Hemingway, who talked for a few minutes. After Hemingway left, Shor asked Berra what he thought of Hemingway. Berra said, "He's OK. What paper does he write for?"

The next morning a special shuttle bus took us from the hotel to Tiger Stadium. We walked past the refreshment stand, full of plump women in white dresses standing over rolling frankfurters, onto the field. Some of the players took time off during batting practice to autograph balls. I thought of all the games I had gone to as a kid and never caught a ball. The closest I ever came was when a man a few rows down from me jumped up and grabbed one, leaving my glove empty. I walked by the National League dugout and noticed a box full of new balls. I wanted to take one, but thought better of it until I noticed several reporters step by the box and take one.

Many players went over to the stands near the dugout and spent five or ten minutes signing autographs before taking batting practice. Everyone strained to get an autograph. People leaned out of the stands and yelled, "Hey, sign mine, sign mine." A player would sign balls, programs, and pieces of paper and then would move off. The crowd then waited for the next player to come into shouting distance.

It was easy for me to get autographs because I was on the field. My ball was getting filled; already I had Tom Seaver, Hank Aaron, Johnny Bench, Willie McCovey, Ron Santo, and Bud Harrelson, but I kept looking around for Willie Mays. When Willie finally appeared at the clubhouse entry he was nearly mobbed by people wanting his autograph. I jumped into the middle of the crowd, pushing and shoving like everyone else till I got my ball autographed.

Soon we were chased off the field and moved up to our press spots. I was assigned to a cage which extended from the second tier right over third base. It was a terrific seat.

The first few innings of the game were crowded with home runs. By the fourth inning the American League had built up a comfortable lead and the game settled into a pitcher's duel. I found myself fingering my autographed ball. I almost took it out and passed it around, wanting to share my prize with the people near me.

By the seventh inning I had stopped taking pictures of the procession of stars and fans and was concentrating on eating franks, drinking beer, and stuffing myself with peanuts. Full of food and the crowd I started daydreaming about the bleachers in Ebbets Field, about home runs Duke Snider used to pole into Flatbush Avenue, and about what a special thing going to a baseball game had been. ■

RICHFIELD, MINNESOTA

UBLY, MICHIGAN

54

ALL-STAR GAME, DETROIT, MICHIGAN

55

ATLANTA, GEORGIA

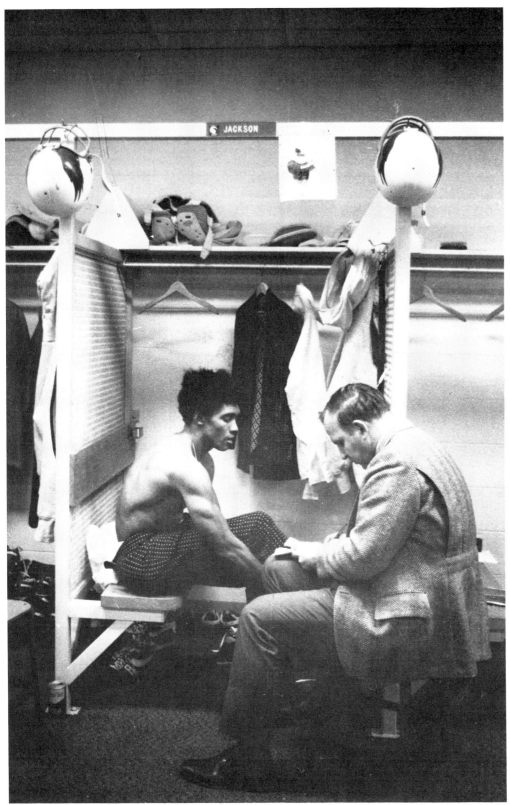

PHILADELPHIA, PENNSYLVANIA

CINCINNATI, OHIO

SYRACUSE, NEW YORK

CHICAGO, ILLINOIS

59

SAN FRANCISCO, CALIFORNIA

CHICAGO, ILLINOIS

60

NEW YORK CITY

NEWSPAPER BOY, YPSILANTI, MICHIGAN

VANCOUVER, WASHINGTON

AMELIA, OHIO

DAYTON, OHIO

NEW HAVEN, CONNECTICUT

TRENTON, NEW JERSEY

68

BUSING TO BEGIN TOMORROW was the headline in Trenton's Sunday paper. When I arrived at Washington School at eight-thirty there was already a cordon of parents carrying all kinds of signs.

The demonstrators had formed two groups. The larger one was marching in front of the school, while a smaller group marched in front of the side entrance, near the teachers' parking lot. Nothing at all was happening in front, but an occasional car with a teacher would get through on the side with the aid of a policeman.

A bus pulled up. All the protesters from both sides of the building moved over to the front of the school, staring at the big yellow school bus with maybe twelve kids in it. All of the little black and Puerto Rican children sat on the far side of the bus away from the chants, signs, and ugly distorted faces.

The bus door opened and three suited men, two white and one black, stepped off, pushed their way through the line, and disappeared into the school. The door closed and the people in front who had stopped walking started up again.

The crowd turned its attention to the eight or ten policemen who had now moved in around the bus. "Why don't you go where there're some criminals, or just get the hell out of here," said one woman.

The police just stood there. After one very vocal woman passed, a young burly cop quietly but audibly said, "Yeah, lady, like we volunteered for this job." And then, even more quietly, he said, "Stupid bitch."

Thirty minutes at least had passed since the three men had gone into the school. Everyone was waiting for decisions, decisions which were to be made downtown.

At one point I was standing on the far side of the bus, away from the school, watching the kids huddled inside, when a man of about fifty-five or sixty came up, his eyes lit with anger, and yelled, "Get out of here, you dirty Communist creep."

I was startled, and said, "What are you talking about?"

He kept on. "Listen, you hippie ass creep, get the fuck out of here before I smash you."

Before I knew it he was kicking at my cameras. The determination was there but the speed was gone. It didn't take too much to keep my cameras out of his way, but I didn't know what to do. Luckily someone I had talked to earlier heard the argument and cooled the man down.

I moved back to the other side of the bus. Still no decisions. Everyone kept walking, waiting for a decision. Finally the three men reappeared from the school and walked past the crowd back onto the bus. They stood inside for a minute and then the bus started its motor and left.

A victory cry arose from the crowd. An 8:30 P.M. meeting was announced to discuss tomorrow's strategy. As I left I heard three women gloating about their victory. One said, "We kept those niggers out, didn't we?" The second said, "No, the colored." The last, laughing, straining to get a high society voice, said, "You mean the people from the predominantly black neighborhood."

I was late for the meeting, which was held in the neighborhood gun and tackle club. The school board wouldn't let them use Washington School. There must have been close to four hundred parents packed into the meeting room, filling every chair, the aisles, and the back area.

Mr. Sparelli was leading the meeting, and was in the midst of explaining the new strategy. He said that the steering committee, of which he was chairman, had decided that instead of blocking the buses they were going to take all of their kids out of the school and just let the bused kids through. "Let them have the school and let's see what they can do with it."

This new strategy got a mixed reaction. Most people seemed less than enthusiastic about the suggestion, but willing to go along with it. However, some parents were visibly upset. A couple of people got up and said that they didn't think that it was a good idea to give the school to the bused kids. "Didn't we stop them today? Why can't we do the same thing tomorrow?"

Finally one lady got up and moved to the front, and said, "Listen, I thought we all agreed we don't want the niggers in our school, so what are we talking about?"

Immediately people said, "Don't talk like that. That isn't what we're here for."

The word "nigger," which was used in the morning, wasn't to be used at this evening's press-covered meeting. The guy next to me explained the change in strategy. The last thing on the early evening news had been a man from the neighborhood saying that if the buses returned the next day they would be overturned.

Mr. Sparelli said, "If anyone touches the buses tomorrow they are going down." He thrust his thick hairy forefinger out at the crowd and said, "I don't care if the person is six foot four, if he touches a bus he is going down with my fist or with a shot in the face. But nobody is going to touch one of them buses tomorrow."

The meeting continued. The next speaker was a police lieutenant, the husband of one of the women on the steering committee. He was given a mixed reception.

In the middle of his talk people started jumping up in the back. Then there were screams, and someone yelled, "There's a fight back here."

The lieutenant left the microphone. Mr. Sparelli started yelling over the microphone, "Sit down, sit down."

Some people sat down but the fight must have gotten larger because the whole back of the room jumped up again.

I noticed that two young guys had moved close to me when the fight started. I said, "Look, I'm not planning to go back there and take pictures of the fight." They smiled and stayed where they were till the fight was moved out into the streets. A lot of people were still standing and Sparelli yelled again, "Sit down, sit down."

One man said, "This is a parents' meeting; get the kids out of here."

Another lady was up. "Yeah, the kids should be at home, not here. My kids are at home, and these kids are going to wreck our meeting." For five minutes adults kept saying that the kids ought to leave. They never did get them all out.

The meeting started again, the chairman explaining that a local tough who was always in trouble had started the fight. The discussion continued as plans were worked out for tomorrow. I left while they were still talking about who would be responsible for calling people, advising them of the plans.

The next morning when I walked over to the school the same women I had chatted with yesterday were there again. The first thing they showed me was the newspaper.

"See," one lady said, "I told you what would happen."

I read the paper quickly, down past the headlines, which said MAYOR SAYS FORCE WILL BE USED IF NECESSARY, to an article that damned those blocking the law. "The law," said the mayor, "will be upheld this morning."

In the next few minutes several people showed me papers. One lady said, "Look, there isn't hardly nothing in this article about what we think, or want. Nobody tells our story, all they do is blast us."

The line in front of the school had grown longer than it had been yesterday. Now there were a lot of kids on the line, not just elementary school-age children, but older kids, high school kids who had obviously skipped school.

A police paddy wagon drove up, and seven or eight policemen got out wearing riot helmets. A murmur of protest and resentment spread through the crowd, the crowd that had promised no violence the night before.

Several of the leaders started talking to the police about the helmets. "What the hell do you think this is? We don't have no riots over here, what's the big idea with these helmets and stuff? Take them off!"

"Sorry, sir, we got our orders downtown."

"I don't give a damn who gave you those goddamn orders, there ain't no riot, take those helmets off!"

After a call downtown the helmets were removed, but the crowd was mad. The helmets had insulted them. What did they think, that they were animals?

All of a sudden there was a screech of brakes and the sound of crashing metal. Everyone started running in the direction of the noise, toward an intersection. You could tell people were nervous and anxious for something to happen. It was just an accident in which one car hadn't turned the corner fast enough, and you couldn't get close enough to see it.

Some ladies had brought a red carpet and laid it out in front of the teachers' parking lot. They had encouraged the teachers not to come to school. Those that did were met with insults as they drove through. Each time a car approached the driveway the women would close in around it, and the two or three policemen would have to move them back.

"Yeah, look how soon you forgot how we backed you when you wanted higher salaries. Shit, you try and ask for more, and see who backs you. Hey, I know her, she's my kid's teacher. My Jerry says good things about you, why do you do this? You just try and ask me for something now."

There was a noise from the front of the school, and everyone raced to the front, watching the yellow bus pull up the road. It didn't stop but went to the corner, turning toward the teachers' parking lot. Everybody raced around the corner again, this time in the other direction. The bus didn't stop at the gate, but passed it, turning around further down the block. Now it started slowly back up the block, turning its nose into the crowd of screaming, placard-carrying parents. For a moment the bus's way was blocked. The two or three policemen at the parking lot were unable to move the crowd. Six more started gently but firmly moving people out of the way.

One woman, looking up at the bus, saw a little girl huddled against the window. Over the din of insults she said, "Don't be scared, we're not going to hurt you, we don't have anything against you."

As these last words came out the bus moved into the courtyard and to the back door. The crowd remained on the other side of the fence, but surged as close to the door as they could. The yellow doors opened and again the three suited men from yesterday stepped off and went into the school. They were followed by six, no, eight policemen who formed a line leading to the door. Then fourteen small children rushed past and into the school.

The crowd moved back onto the street. A man almost got in a fight with one of the policemen, who was foolishly pushing a point. All the men around who weren't satisfied by yelling at the kids started joining in. The policeman was confused, but wouldn't back down. Before anything more than raised voices happened another policeman moved in, sent the first one away, and soothed the feelings of the crowd.

Another bus passed by, headed for some other neighborhood school and similar treatment. The crowd turned its noise on the bus as it passed, and a little black boy in the back of the bus looked around, and then stuck out his pink tongue till the bus was out of sight. ■

TAOS, NEW MEXICO

ROXBURY, MASSACHUSETTS

74

NEW HAVEN, CONNECTICUT

ROUTE 70, TENNESSEE

TAOS, NEW MEXICO

NAVAJO RESERVATION, WINDOW ROCK, ARIZONA

WINDOW ROCK, ARIZONA

MONTGOMERY, ALABAMA

While I was watching some kids play, a man wandered into the park. He wasn't old but he certainly wasn't young. I wouldn't have called him a bum, but it would have been more than kind to call his clothes casual.

He walked around the tiny park for a while, finally stopping by a tree stump. As soon as he had sat down, he got up and moved to a torn sofa. He leaned back into the sofa, his left foot loosely draped over his right, and took a bottle of cold duck out of a brown paper bag. He took two quick swigs and returned the bottle to the bag. He looked over at the kids playing on the jungle gym and swings. When they left, he rolled a cigarette and sat farther back into the sofa, the top of his head resting on the back of the sofa. When he had finished the cigarette he crushed the butt with his sandal, sat up erectly, took the cold duck out again, and had two long swallows.

He didn't lean back. Instead he got up and walked over to the swings. He paused in front of them for a long minute, and then placing his hands

on the edge of the swing's seat he pulled it back close to his body and held it there. Then he opened his hands and the swing swung freely until he caught it and held it up just as he had before. This time when he released it, he gave it a push, then another, then a third. As it swung, he moved down the line of swings and first with a foot and then with a hand he started each of the three, setting them all into motion.

He moved back to the sofa. He sat with his feet stretched into the dirt in front of him and finished the cold duck. He held the empty bottle up, looking at it for a while in the same halting way that he had looked at the swing. Then he put the bottle back in the brown paper bag and buried it beneath a pile of newspapers in a large wire trash barrel.

He sat down again only long enough to roll himself another cigarette, and then he started walking. As he passed the swings, he pushed each one into motion without hesitation. They kept swinging as he walked across the street and out of view. ■

81

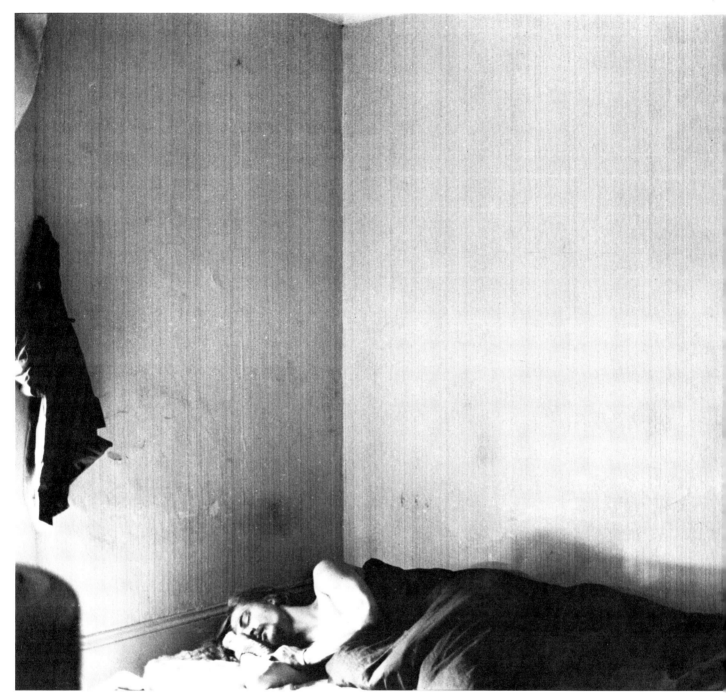

PORTLAND, MAINE

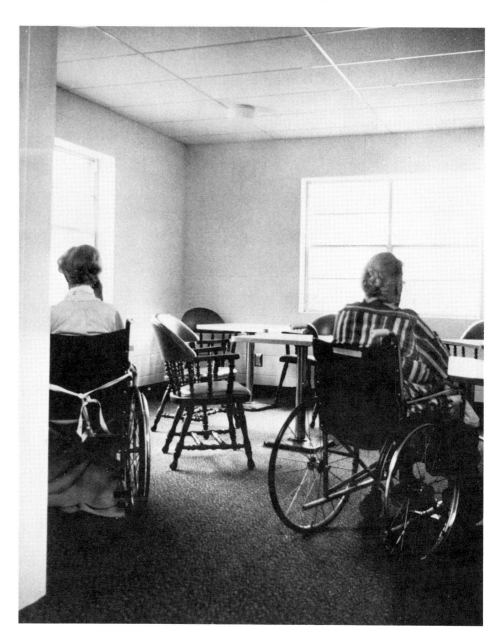

MOBILE, ALABAMA

NEW ORLEANS, LOUISIANA

PHILADELPHIA, PENNSYLVANIA

MINNEAPOLIS, MINNESOTA

PHOENIX, ARIZONA

86

TRURO, CAPE COD, MASSACHUSETTS

87

BLACK PANTHER FUNERAL, OAKLAND, CALIFORNIA

MEMORIAL DAY SERVICES, MIDWEST CITY, OKLAHOMA

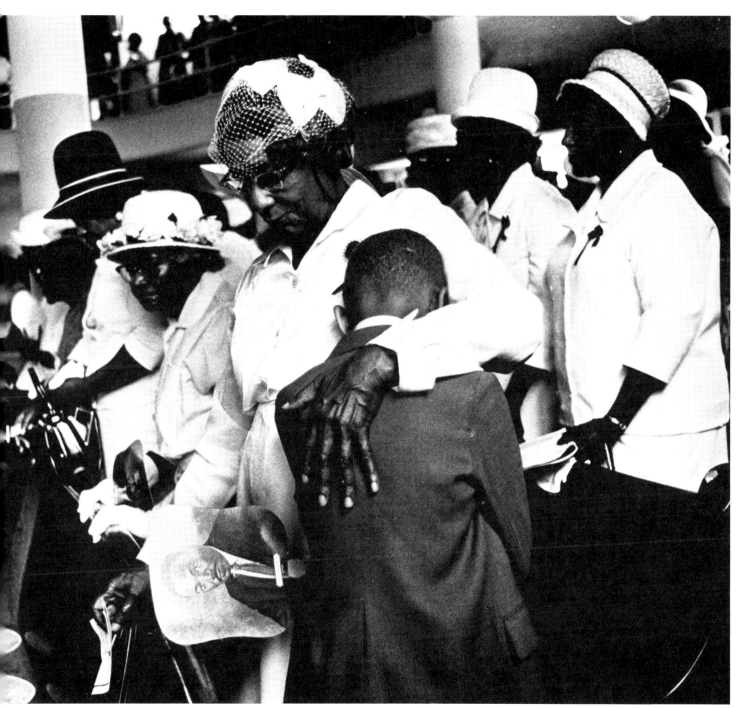

FUNERAL, CLEVELAND, OHIO

89

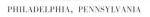
PHILADELPHIA, PENNSYLVANIA

INDIANAPOLIS, INDIANA

PHOENIX, ARIZONA

90

NEW ORLEANS, LOUISIANA

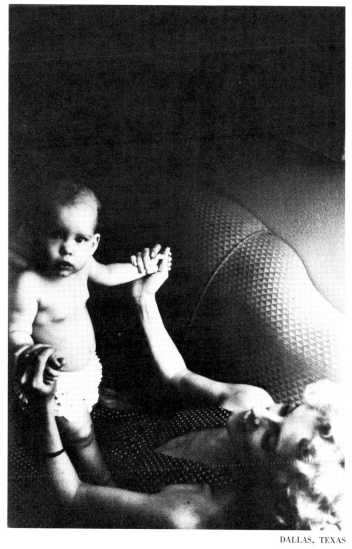

DALLAS, TEXAS

93

Will was standing with a sign in his hand which read "New York" when I picked him up on the road outside Tucson, Arizona. I told him I could take him as far as Dallas. It was going to be a long drive so we took turns driving. When I drove Will would slouch real low in the other seat, resting his sneakers on the windshield. Once he pulled a harmonica out of his pocket, played it for a while, and then held it out the window letting the wind make its own tune.

Will began talking about how beautiful Canada was, and how maybe before he went East he would head down into Mexico. Then all of a sudden he said, "I'm not really going to New York. I'm going to Lewisburg, Pennsylvania. You see, my best friend lives there. That is, we were best friends. I don't know now . . . I've got to straighten things out with him.

"His name is Ted. We were best friends during high school. When I took to the road three years ago he went off to college. He's done real well—made Phi Beta Kappa. The beautiful thing was we weren't competitive. We respected each other and shared everything. Like last summer we took a trip into the Nevada desert. No car, just a canteen of water and some grass. It was fabulous. We started by sharing a couple of joints and ended up sharing the little water we had. Each drop became precious. The whole trip was like that, every minute precious.

"But somehow he changed. A couple of months ago I hitched up from Florida to see him. He was unreal. He kept coming down on me about everything. It got so bad that I was even afraid to open the refrigerator and eat anything. He was making me feel incredibly uptight and insecure, so I split for the West Coast.

"I got a few crummy rides and hadn't gone very far when I spotted some guys I had seen around Lehigh at a turnpike gas station. They said they were going to Denver, so I asked if I could go along. I squeezed in the back. There were four of them; they were fraternity brothers. They turned the radio up real loud and took off down the highway drinking beer, smoking, and bragging about different girls. Somehow, I couldn't get into it, so I curled up in a corner.

"Occasionally they would jerk the car off the road to piss. The third time they did it Al, the guy driving, turned and said, 'Listen, Will, the car can't make it with all this weight. You'll have to get out.'

"There I was at two-thirty in the morning on the highway in the middle of Ohio. I sat on my suitcase for nearly five hours watching a series of headlights go past before I got another ride. It took me about three days to get to California, but it was worth it. After a while I regained my self-confidence and headed East again to settle things with Ted."

Just then a young hitchhiker was momentarily caught in my headlights. For a few seconds after I stopped there was only the sound of feet running on gravel, and then a young boy lifted himself up into the front seat. He and Will started talking almost immediately. Tired of talk, I started thinking about home and how much I wanted to be off the road and with Eileen. Finally I realized I had missed a turn, stopped, let the new kid off, and turned around.

"Where's the kid going?" I asked Will.

"You won't believe this, Dick, but I think he's running away from home. He said he was going to Amarillo but he doesn't have any idea where it is. And while we were talking I told him I left home when I was eighteen. He told me he was only sixteen."

I turned the van around, thinking maybe we should talk to the kid. I felt awkward as we approached him, unsure of what to say. For the first time I took a good look at him. He looked younger than sixteen. He was small and homely-looking and clutching a paper bag under his arm.

I said, "Look, we'd like to talk to you for a couple of minutes. Why don't you come back inside the van?"

He looked suspicious, but without saying a word followed us back into the front seat.

"Where you going?" I asked.

"Amarillo, sir."

"Do you know how far it is from here?"

"Yes, sir, seventy miles."

"Come on, Amarillo is over two hundred miles and you're on the wrong road. Look," I continued, "we aren't cops. If you want to run away from home, it's your own business. But it's silly to leave this late at night and pick such a lonely road to travel on."

"I ain't running away, sir. I'm going home."

I pulled a Texas map out of the glove compartment. He looked at it and said, "Maybe I better get on another road."

"You know," I said, "you could spend the night with us and we'd put you on the road for Amarillo in the morning."

His beady eyes looked up with fear and he said, "No, thank you, sir. I'll just start hitching again."

He opened the door and swung back down to the shoulder of the road. We turned around once again and left him standing there in the darkness. I was upset. I wanted to know what he was running from, where he was going, and how we might help him. I didn't want to think that what he wanted was for us to leave him alone.

We began looking for a place to sleep and settled on a small park. Will, who had been silent for a long time, now said, "You know, maybe I'll leave for home tonight."

I told him it didn't make sense to me, but if he wanted to he should.

"Yeah, I guess it doesn't make sense," he admitted. "I guess I'll get some sleep and hit the road real early before you get up."

Late the next afternoon just before we reached Dallas Will said, "You know, maybe I'll go see Dallas. I've never been there."

"Look, Will," I said, "I've got work to do in Dallas. I'm staying with people I don't really know and I just can't take you along."

"How about if I stay in the van at night?"

"No, Will, it just won't work. I can't take you with me."

"All right," he said. "Anyway, I ought to get going or I'll never get to Lewisburg. How about giving me a lift to the highway?" ■

96

CHICAGO, ILLINOIS

COLORADO

97

BERKELEY, CALIFORNIA

I was just riding around when I saw this little girl riding her tricycle.
I stopped and took some pictures of her. At first she paid no attention
to me, but finally she asked, "What are you doing?"

I answered, "Taking pictures."

My answer must not have satisfied her because she asked, "But why
are you taking them?"

"Well," I said, "because you look like a witch."

"Oh," she said, "I am a witch, and there's another one who lives
up the block." ■

BERKELEY, CALIFORNIA

BROWNWOOD, TEXAS

VANCOUVER, WASHINGTON

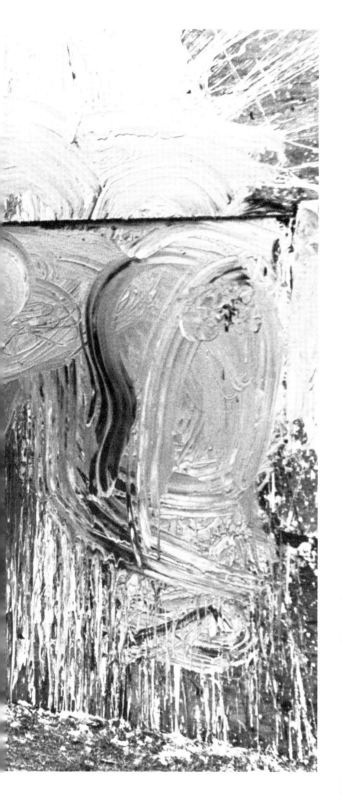

YPSILANTI, MICHIGAN

PHILADELPHIA, PENNSYLVANIA

NEW ORLEANS, LOUISIANA

BOSTON, MASSACHUSETTS

RACE TRACK, ARLINGTON, ILLINOIS

PERFECTA
$2

SALEM, OREGON

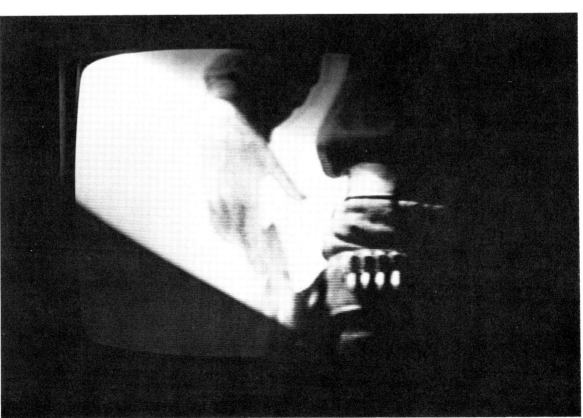

TV SCREEN, LINCOLN, MASSACHUSETTS

TUCSON, ARIZONA

PORTLAND, OREGON

111

AMERICAN LEGION CONVENTION, PORTLAND, OREGON

CENTRAL CITY, COLORADO

113

ELLENSBURG, WASHINGTON

ELLENSBURG, WASHINGTON

On the sign in the image:
M. UP TO $50.00 $4.00
"$50.00 UP TO $100.00 $5.00
"$100.00 UP ‾ $6.00
EED $1.00 DAY
M. O...STOCK 5%
AL...   .00 EACH

CHAIRS RESERVED
FOR BUYERS

HORSE AUCTION, SOUTHWEST GEORGIA

I walked around the dirt pit of the rodeo arena noticing that up close cowboys look a lot different than from arena seats, or on TV, or in the movies. They look more as though they come from the pages of *Mad* Magazine than from the billboards of Marlboro country. Several hadn't shaved, a number walked with noticeable limps, others had wrists, hands, and even arms bandaged.

Most of the cowboys stood around the inner wall of the arena in little clusters. At one point I found myself in the midst of a group of five or six of them. They talked past me, over me, around me, so I moved away from them, farther down the wall. I sat down near an unshaven cowboy.

He was wearing a flat gray hat and had a toothpick sticking out of a browned set of teeth, his eyes hidden behind thick bifocal glasses. I tried to work up a conversation.

"Are you in an event?"

"Yup." That's all he said. Yup.

"Which one?" I asked.

"Calf wrestling."

"Oh, really? How long you been doing it?"

"Six years."

"Well, how old were you when you started?"

"Huh, oh, nineteen."

I couldn't think of anything else to ask so we sat there in silence for a good ten minutes before, much to my surprise, he started talking, the toothpick moving up and down as he spit the words out of the right side of his mouth. He said that he attended about thirty rodeos a year. His specialty was calf wrestling.

Each contestant is charged a $50 entrance fee. The rider with the top time for two rides over the three days gets $1,000. The rider with the best time each day gets some money too. This cowboy averaged between $3,000 and $5,000 a year from the rodeo. Once, three years ago, he had made $8,000.

I asked why he stayed with the rodeo. He shook his head and said, "I don't know. It ain't a bad living. Anyway, I don't know what else I would do. My dad was a national champion so I guess everyone always sort of expected me to go into the rodeo. Used to be I would put about $1,000 a year away. Hell, now I'm lucky to put anything away, but I like it, and like I said it's what I know."

We fell back into silence and watched the calf roping. "Next event, calf wrestling," called the voice over the PA. The cowboy next to me jumped up, used his hat to brush the dirt off his breeches, and disappeared behind the chutes.

I watched the entire calf wrestling competition waiting to see the guy I had talked with. He was one of the last contestants. He had a very good time. In fact, he posted the best time of the day.

Only one event left: steer riding. The arena area near the steer riding chutes was already crowded with photographers. One cowboy leaning against the fence yelled, "I hope you get your fool ass a little closer so the steer can kick it." The photographers moved back.

Each time the door is yanked open the animal comes hurtling out with a great leap, landing only long enough to spin and leap again, jarring the rider up into the air, his legs flapping, his hand straining on the rope that holds him to the steer's back. The gravel spits out from under the steer's legs as it kicks them high in the air.

I watched from a safe distance, trying to take a good picture, but I was too far away. I moved closer but I didn't know where to stand. It must have been obvious. A cowboy came over and showed me a spot, telling me that when the gate swung back, the steer would take a step in my direction and then spin to the left. I positioned myself, set my camera, and figured out the angle for the shot I wanted.

All of a sudden the chute opened. The steer stepped out just as the cowboy had said it would, but it didn't spin to the left, it spun to the right, closer to me. I saw just enough of its spin to start one of my own. As I hit the first rail of the fence, a hand grabbed my back and turned me around. The steer had passed the spot where I had been standing before turning back the other way. The cowboy who had positioned me was laughing his head off, moving down the line of cowboys and talking about what had just happened. ■

PHILADELPHIA, PENNSYLVANIA

120

PORTLAND, OREGON

PHILADELPHIA, PENNSYLVANIA

EVANSTON, ILLINOIS

121

SANTA FE, NEW MEXICO

123

MARDI GRAS, NEW ORLEANS, LOUISIANA

124

PORTLAND, OREGON

PORTLAND, OREGON

PORTLAND, OREGON

125

BOSTON, MASSACHUSETTS

HIDDEN LAKE, MONTANA

Hidden Lake was something I had wanted to see for a long time, so when I entered Glacier National Park I eagerly climbed to Logan Pass to find it. Since I only had summer clothes with me, I hesitated at the bottom of the 2-mile snow-covered path to the lake. Hell, I thought, two miles really isn't that far, and so I started up the path past the first marker and a group of warmly dressed people coming down.

I couldn't have walked more than a half a mile before I felt myself breathing heavily. But I kept moving, already beginning to feel the wetness of the snow pass through my boots and socks to my toes. I tried not to pay attention to my discomfort by playing a little game; I would carefully walk in the footprints of people who had gone by earlier. I kept walking, occasionally looking back at the chalet at Logan Pass. When the chalet had just about disappeared I was certain that it couldn't be much farther.

My thighs felt the weight of the climb up the snowy crest. I was no longer taking long straight steps. My feet were now turned outward and I was managing only short uneven steps. When I reached the top

128

of the incline I didn't find Hidden Lake but a new expanse of snow-covered ground in front of me.

I thought of turning back, for I could feel sweat on my chest and the need to rest. I reasoned with myself that this wasn't a John Wayne movie and that I had nothing to prove. All I had to do was turn around and move back to the warmth of the chalet.

But I kept walking, knowing the lake couldn't be but a short distance away. Now I was in heavy snow, and the footprints so easy to follow earlier seemed to sink and disappear. I walked a little farther and spotted some pine bushes, behind which I was sure I would find the lake. I walked a little faster, stiff with cold, but anxious to see Hidden Lake, to mock it and myself for this needlessly tortuous walk.

But there was another slope beyond the pines. It was useless to turn back now; I had gone too far. I needed to finish, and so cursing myself for starting this trip I pushed on until I reached the end of the trail. There in front of me was an incredible drop, and below was Hidden Lake.

I stood there in the absolute quiet for a very long time hearing only the cool rush of air. ■

SAN FRANCISCO, CALIFORNIA

132

NEW YORK CITY

PHILADELPHIA, PENNSYLVANIA

MARINA DEL REY, CALIFORNIA

INDIANA TURNPIKE

CHICAGO, ILLINOIS

CINCINNATI, OHIO

CINCINNATI, OHIO

136

FORT LAUDERDALE, FLORIDA

MEN'S ROOM, FLORIDA

137

LUMPKIN, GEORGIA

The Bridgetons—friends of a friend—live about 5 miles outside of Lumpkin, Georgia, a small southern courthouse town. Louise Bridgeton greeted me at the door and ushered me into the living room where we sat sipping beer and talking. From time to time our conversation was interrupted by her two daughters, who kept dancing in and out of the room.

Even with these interruptions Louise began telling me about Lumpkin. "You probably won't believe this, Richard, but just this past year there were several public places which still wouldn't serve black people. A local drugstore took out their counter service rather than integrate and people are still afraid to test whether Sadie will integrate her motel.

"Richard," she continued, "that isn't the worst of it. We still haven't integrated the schools. That's right. Hell, a lot of other towns which have integrated have set up private academies so the white kids won't need to go to school with black kids. This town doesn't even have an academy."

We talked for a while longer and then I told Louise that I thought I would visit the private cue club she had mentioned. She looked surprised but then said maybe it would be OK. "But!" she added, "I can't say I won't worry about you. They say there are a lot of fights there, and there's no telling what might happen. So you got to promise to be careful." As I got up to leave Louise said that if I didn't return by midnight she and her father would come looking for me.

I drove into town, parked the van, and walked up to the poolroom. I swung the screen door open and walked through the wooden door into a large, well-lit room containing three pool tables with overhead fluorescent lights. Only one of the tables was being used. I stood around for a minute or two, surprised that no one came up asking me what I was doing. When I realized that I would probably be totally ignored unless I did something, I walked up to the four guys who were playing pool and asked if they would mind if I took some pictures. They looked at each other for a minute, and then one of them said he didn't think any of them cared but I ought to ask Little John, the owner, who was in the bar area in the back.

I thanked them and walked back past the plaster partition into the small, dimly lit bar area, which was nothing more than an L-shaped counter ringed by a dozen stools. I asked the bartender if he was Little John. I was hoping he wasn't, for no other reason than that he looked like a squashed Lennie from *Of Mice and Men*. But of course he was. I introduced myself, explained that I was a photographer passing through town, and that I was wondering if he would mind if I took some pictures in the bar. He looked at me silently for a time, and then said, "You can stay in the bar, but don't take any pictures."

I started to ask why, but thought the better of it and just said, "OK." I sat down not knowing exactly what I would do next, when a man asked if he could buy me a beer. Just what I needed. His name was Martin. He was sixty-six, had graying but not yet white hair and a white stubble beard. "I heard you talking to Little John," he said.

You know, I've done a lot of traveling myself. Been all around the world. I did a lot of things before coming back home. Now I take care of my brother's land."

Martin was sitting on my right, and while we talked he introduced me to Fred, who was sitting on my left. Before long the three of us were yapping away. Just after we started on our second beer Martin bragged that he had done everything imaginable during his life, but two things.

"What's that?" I asked.

"I haven't fathered me a nigger baby, and I haven't saved any money." Fred laughed, and I smiled, trying not to look too self-conscious. Somehow what Martin had said started Fred talking about some "nigger MP" who patrols around Fort Benning, thirty miles northeast of Lumpkin. The more Fred talked about the MP the angrier he became. He started in a rather mild voice, saying, "There's this one nigger MP who stops women driving through the military reservation and gives them a hard time. Shit," he added, "he wouldn't stop the women if there were any men in the car."

Fred had worked himself up, and had to move his hand across his mouth to wipe the wetness away from his lips before continuing. "If that son of a bitch ever stops any women from my family I'll blow his mother-fuckin' head off."

When I had finished my beer I got up to leave. Martin had agreed to show me his brother's farm the next morning. Fred didn't say anything but followed me outside, and said I could stay at his house. No sooner had I said no thanks than Fred started in again. "Nope," he said, "I have no use for niggers. I had to work hard for what I made, not like them

139

niggers." He leaned close to me, his liquor breath on my face, and continued. "When I got hurt I couldn't get shit from the state. I wouldn't want anything from the government anyway, but if one of those niggers got hurt you'd see just how much he would get."

I had had enough. I walked across the street. Fred was still following me so I didn't turn around till I had climbed into the van, turned on the engine, and moved down the road.

Louise and her father were still up. I told them about the bar and the people I had met. Louise's father, Ralph, said Martin was like most white people in town. But Fred, he was something else. Fred, Ralph said, was crazy. "No, sir," Ralph said, "don't go messing with Fred; he's crazy. Fred will fool you because he drinks a lot. People don't take him serious but that man knows exactly what he's doing and he'll hurt you."

Later, a hard, driving rain, pounding on the top of the van, woke me up. I pulled myself out of the sleeping bag, threw on some clothes, and found Martin just as he was backing his Ford pickup out of his driveway. The rain had let up a little, but Martin complained that the weather was aggravating his arthritis. "Not a fit day," Martin said, "for a white man to be out."

We rode out Route 27 past large tracts of flat, fertile land, man-made ponds, and the remains of plantation tenant homes in which people still lived. Martin turned off the engine at his brother's farm, pointed around, and said, "Yup, we own more than eighteen hundred acres. We lease almost all of it now, but it's still ours."

It was early afternoon when we got back to Lumpkin. I thanked Martin and went back out to the Bridgetons, where Ralph and his son-in-law were in the midst of slaughtering a couple of pigs. I watched for a while and then drove back into town to watch a basketball game on the color TV in the poolroom. No one from last night was in the bar.

During the half I went outside to take a picture of the Members Only sign. I pushed the screen door open, holding it with my foot, and took three quick shots, put my camera away, and walked back into the bar.

Not five minutes of the second half had gone by before I noticed people leaving the bar for a minute or two, going not to the bathroom but the other side of the partition. I had a queer feeling that something was wrong, but I thought I was being ridiculous. I took a swig of beer, and concentrated on the game. Then someone from the other side of the partition started calling Helen, Little John's Wife.

"I can't come," Helen yelled. "I'm busy."

"Come on, Helen, just for a minute."

"OK, OK," she said, as she threw down the cloth she was using to clean off the bar. I started getting nervous again. Suppose someone had seen my van behind the Bridgetons'.

When Helen returned behind the bar she didn't pick up her cloth. Instead she glanced over at me. I tried to act cool and unconcerned, even when she came over, looked at me, and matter-of-factly said, "Did you take any pictures outside?"

"Yes," I said.

"How come?" she asked. "I thought my husband asked you not to take any pictures of this place."

"Ma'am," I politely said, "your husband told me he didn't want any pictures taken in here, and I haven't taken any."

"My husband didn't want any pictures taken."

"Well, I have kept my word, I haven't taken any pictures in here." The conversation ended when she said, "The reason I ask all this is because some people are curious about what you are doing."

Saying that, Helen turned back to her cloth and wiping the bar. I turned back to the TV and watched Notre Dame beat a highly favored UCLA. The whole time I was mad at myself. How dumb could I be? What I had just done was bound to make them suspicious.

After the game I went back out to the Bridgetons for dinner. Ralph said grace and then we dug into the fried chicken, mashed potatoes, salad, and peaches. It all disappeared pretty quickly. After dinner Ralph suggested we go to a private club up the road and shoot some pool. Ralph, his son Robert, his son-in-law Joe, and I piled into Ralph's car.

We took the lock off the clubhouse door, put some wood into the potbellied stove, and turned on the lights. It was decided that our playing would improve greatly if we had something to drink. Each of us kicked in a couple of bucks and Joe went off to get some gin and soda.

We played sort of round robin. The winner could keep the table as long as he won. But when Ralph had beaten both Robert and me a couple of times he let Robert and me play each other. Joe must have been gone for about fifty minutes before he reappeared. When he came in he wasn't carrying any liquor. He spoke quietly, looking at Ralph the whole time he talked. He said, "I think you better come home."

Ralph, who was in the middle of a game with Robert, held up his cue for a minute, looked at Joe, smiled, and said that when we were finished playing we would go home.

Joe looked at Ralph and repeated, "I think you better come home."

I couldn't understand why Ralph didn't sense the urgency in Joe's voice. He kept playing, and only said, "After the game, Joe."

"You better come *now*," Joe said. "There's a warrant or something down at the house."

There wasn't a sound in the room, except for the crackling of burning wood. Joe broke the silence, saying, "I couldn't make much sense of the paper, but Louise said you better come home."

Ralph put on his jacket while Robert and I stood around, unsure of what to do. Joe turned to us and said, "I think you both better come too." We mechanically closed things up and went back to the car.

Not another word was said till we pulled in the driveway. Joe hadn't done more than step on the brake before Ralph was out of the car and headed inside. The kitchen was crowded. Ralph's wife was holding a piece of crumpled paper. Louise and Candy, Robert's wife, were standing around. Ralph looked at the paper and handed it to me. To my surprise it wasn't

141

a warrant. It was a summons ordering Ralph to appear in court February 26 about an outstanding bill of $28.35 at a local store.

As I explained the difference between a warrant and a summons Ralph took the paper out of my hand. He studied it this time and then said, looking around the room, "I'm not going to study this. No, sir, I'm just going to put it into my pocket." And he did just that.

Everyone moved from the center of the room to the nearest chair, stool, or table top. Ralph asked Joe to break out some drinks and then began asking Louise and his wife about the summon's server. Neither Louise nor her mother had recognized the man. "No," Louise said, "he wasn't anyone we know hardly at all. He drove up, knocked on the door, and mumbled some name, maybe it was Richard, but I know he never said Ralph." Then, looking at her father, she continued, "Now everyone around these parts knows your name good enough."

Ralph's wife said, "that debt is more than a year old. Why did they wait till now, late Saturday night, to deliver it?"

Ralph did most of the talking as we went over and over the details about the summons server. He took the paper out of his pocket, looked at it, struck his palm on it, and said, "If they think with the little bit I get on a VA pension that I'm going to pay this bill, they're crazy. Shoot, I'm just not going to pay attention to this." This time he didn't fold it up as he stuffed it back into his shirt. I wanted to interrupt Ralph and say, "Look, let's talk about why the summons is bothering you so much." But I didn't feel I had the right to do that, so I sat there quietly instead.

Before long Louise got up and said good night. Then Robert and his wife got up and said good night, having neither finished their drinks nor said a word since we returned to the house. Ralph, sitting there drinking his gin, pulled the piece of paper out of his pocket again. He didn't look at it this time, just held it. He said, "The money I make is for my kids and their food, and I'll be damned if I'm going to take money out of their mouths for this kind of thing." No one said a word. Ralph kept talking. "I get another check next month and I'll bring it down there and they can take the money out if they want." Now he asked, "Do you think they'll do anything further about the debt?" Still no one said anything. Ralph put the paper back in his pocket, saying, "I don't think they'd put me in jail if I don't pay."

Later, when the others had left, Ralph and I sat in the kitchen facing each other on either side of a small potbellied stove that warmed not only the kitchen but a good part of the house. Ralph took off his glasses. He took one look at me and then started talking about his life.

He talked about being a child in the South during the Depression. "I had to take all kinds of jobs to get by. I've done a little of everything. I worked on a farm at the end of the Depression, worked on heavy machinery and done a lot of other things just to get by. But my specialty was cooking, which I learned a lot better when I went into the service."

He talked about the Army, discrimination, the VA pension he had and about how tough it was making ends meet. He got up to fill our glasses again, checked the ribs he was cooking, and returned to his seat.

Somehow he began talking about this house. He said that he owned eleven acres of land which had cost him $1,600. You couldn't buy that many acres now for twice, maybe even three times the money. He had bought all the material for the house, having stored some of it in the house they had lived in before. He had lumber worth $12,000. He put up his own aluminum siding for $4,600 and it cost him $1,200 to dig a well. It had taken the family over a year to actually build the house, even after they had all the supplies.

It wasn't quite finished. He looked around, pointing at things that still needed to be done. "Still," he said, "I think I've done all right, and my children and grandchildren will enjoy it even if I can't."

He continued. "The smartest thing I did was not taking a mortgage from a local bank. I took a mortgage from a black bank up in Atlanta and knew I wouldn't be cheated. I never would miss a payment. No, I've never missed a payment, and," he added with his face stretched toward mine, "I would do almost anything before I'd give this place up."

He went over to the fire again and said the ribs were done. We packed them away, cleaning the sauce from our fingers and leaving just the bones.

Ralph got up, said he was tired and was going to go to sleep. He left me by my room, walked to the kitchen, took a shot of gin, and disappeared into the bathroom. He reappeared long enough to remove some false teeth and extend his hand to say good night. ■

LUMPKIN, GEORGIA

GREAT NECK, NEW YORK

144

BENEVOLENCE, GEORGIA

145

146

FAITH HEALER, DONALSONVILLE, GEORGIA

HARVARD LAW SCHOOL, CAMBRIDGE, MASSACHUSETTS

OAKLAND, CALIFORNIA

PHILADELPHIA, PENNSYLVANIA

149

HIGHLAND PARK, ILLINOIS

DEERFIELD, ILLINOIS

PHILADELPHIA, PENNSYLVANIA

CHICAGO, ILLINOIS

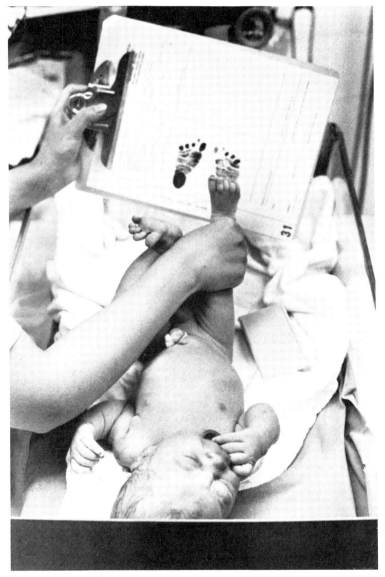

PHILADELPHIA, PENNSYLVANIA

153

GOVERNOR WALLACE'S INAUGURATION, MONTGOMERY, ALABAMA

MARDI GRAS BALL, MOBILE, ALABAMA

GRADUATION, NORTHWESTERN UNIVERSITY, EVANSTON, ILLINOIS

DAYTON, OHIO

For the past eighteen years Altoona has been the site of the Jaycee-sponsored Miss Central Pennsylvania pageant. The winner here goes on to the state competition and possibly the Miss America pageant in Atlantic City. According to the official program a Miss America winner at the local or national level

> . . .is NOT a beauty queen. She is an intelligent young woman who possesses dignity, poise, charm, good manners, beauty, talent and the intangible called personality . . . she must be able to meet the public, speak extemporaneously, and represent her city and state with dignity and youthful charm. She must also have the necessary beauty and wholesomeness to appeal to the American public.

Ten girls, little numbers attached to their clothes, were waiting nervously outside a small conference room at the Penn Alto Hotel for the final judging to begin. Inside the room were three of the judges.

While we waited I talked with judge Joe Ristagno. Ristagno, who owns a bakery and works as an interior decorator, is not new to either judging or pageants. I asked him what he looks for in the girls.

"Personality," he said. "The way I figure it, a girl can learn one song on the piano and play it well in the talent competition, but she can't carry the piano around the state with her. She's got to be able to talk and make a good impression."

"Do you find judging talent difficult?" I asked.

"No, not really. People think it's hard because a judge can't really be familiar with all types of talent. But I know what I like and I know what's good."

Joe introduced me to another judge, Father Tom Smith, pastor of a small suburban congregation in Roscoe, Pennsylvania. Father Tom, as he liked to be called, was wearing a well-tailored belted sport jacket with suppressed waist, tapered trousers, and even a collar that seemed form-fitting. Before I could ask him any questions the last judge arrived, and David Harp, the Jaycee man in charge of judges, assembled everyone for a pre-interview briefing.

"The interview," David said, "is very important because it will give you your first real impression of the girls. We are limiting the interview to five minutes and at that time no matter where the interview is you must cut it off. Feel free to ask the girls anything you want, but I can't permit any political or religious questions."

The first girl was brought in and introduced to the judges, who were now seated behind a long table. She sat a few feet in front of them on a metal chair. No pressure, just friendly questions about her family, why she liked the piano, and what type of career she wanted. Finally David Harp, who was seated well behind the girl with a stopwatch in his hand, thrust his left arm high in the air, signaling that the five minutes were almost up. Less than thirty seconds later he made a cutting gesture and Father Tom said, "I'm sorry, your time is up, thank you very much."

Several more girls, and more questions about brothers and sisters, interests and career plans. Then Toni came in. She was not thin and bouncy like most of the other girls. She was less effervescent, more a woman than a girl. She was, in fact, plump and several years older than the other contestants. The first question she was asked was, "Why have you waited so long to compete?"

"Do you mean why am I so old?" she answered.

The judges laughed and then began asking Toni the usual questions about family, career, and ambitions. Toni said she had no ambition to become a great opera star. She said, "I like teaching at a small college and giving an occasional recital." When she left one judge remarked, "She has a great attitude, I wish it would flow down to her body."

When the interviews were finished I hurried downstairs, hoping to talk with some of the girls before the banquet dinner. Several of the girls were standing around with their Jaycette chaperones. I asked what kind of suggestions the chaperones had made to the girls. One girl said that her hands always sweat when she's nervous, and her chaperone had advised her to use Arrid extra-dry deodorant on her palms. "It works" she said.

Dinner consisted of turkey, stuffing, string beans, and was followed by speeches in which everyone connected with the pageant was thanked for his contribution.

Just as the ice cream dessert was being served Jean Walters, last year's Miss Central Pennsylvania and fourth runner-up at the state pageant, was introduced. She stood, smiled, and then, her voice close to breaking, began speaking.

"Tonight is a very sad time for me, for it ends the best year of my life. For all the people that made my last year possible there aren't enough words to express my gratitude. Thank you, thank you, thank you all."

There was a round of applause. Jean looked around the room at this year's contestants and continued. "I want all you girls who are running to know you are all marvelous, you are all wonderful, and you are all winners in your own way. And to everyone, God bless."

Soon dinner was over, and nearly everyone rushed off for last-minute adjustments. I grabbed Duane Burdell, the man in charge of the entire pageant. I asked him if any of the Miss Central Pennsylvania girls had ever become Miss Pennsylvania. He said, "No, but in the five years I've been director three of our girls have been in the top five. To be honest," he continued, "my ambition is to place one of our girls first in the state competition.

"You can't realize how much there is to do. We start by encouraging girls to compete. This year twenty-six girls tried out. We had preliminaries and ten girls were selected for final competition. Then we work with the girls for more than ten weeks and I'll tell you, Dick, that's why tonight you're going to see a show. It's a show that much bigger pageants don't have. I think I can honestly say our production is as good as if not better than what you'll see at the state pageant at Hershey, and to my way of thinking you won't see a more professional show, not even at Atlantic City."

The pageant was being held at the Shriners' mosque. There were only a thousand people there and they didn't even begin to fill up the auditorium. The disappointing turnout was in part due to two competing events, an annual Rotary dinner and a professional wrestling match.

The MC was John Riley, a celebrity, the weatherman of the local TV station. All night John kept the program moving smoothly along. The first number was announced, "It gives me great pleasure to introduce Father Tom Smith. Father Tom is serving in a dual capacity tonight, as judge and entertainer. He has just completed a successful taping of the 'Mike Douglas Show' and has toured all around the country with his program which he calls 'Him, Hymn, and Me.' Ladies and gentlemen, it is my pleasure to introduce to you Father Tom Smith, the singing and dancing priest."

The curtain opened and there was Father Tom decked out in a black tapered evening suit with velvet lapels and cuffs. Father Tom, microphone in hand and teeth ablaze, began singing about a priest who wanted to sing and dance. His undulating hips and nightclub leg-kicks were a big success with the audience. By the time the ten finalists had burst through tissue paper barriers and done a little choreographed number, the crowd was generously applauding. A woman in front of me whispered, "Why can't *we* have a priest like that?"

"Now," John Riley said, "we begin tonight's competition. There will be the gown, swimsuit, and talent competition." The gown and swimsuit competition were very similar. The girls walked down the runway once in evening gowns, the other time in bathing suits. Of the two, the bathing suit competition captured much more of the crowd's interest. The photographers rushed to the runway. After each girl had walked down the runway all ten stood on a platform above the judges, who were looking for the following things: 1) hourglass figure, 2) legs, 3) knees, 4) thighs, 5) tummy, 6) back and spine curvature, 7) shoulder blades, 8) neck, 9) face and head (teeth, ears, hair).

They must have been having a tough time. After the girls had made a full turn, a quarter turn at a time, David Harp asked if any of them wanted the girls to make any more turns. The judges said yes, and the girls made two additional quarter turns before leaving.

Each girl was given two and one half minutes for her talent. I couldn't see the judges' ratings, but I used a rating system from 1–10 and didn't give anyone above a 7½. My 7½ went to Toni, who sang an aria from an opera. I would have given her a higher mark but I don't like opera. I gave another girl, who played a Grieg piano piece, a 7. One girl did a death scene from *Anne of the Thousand Days.* I gave her a 2 after twenty-five seconds and might have raised it to 4 if she hadn't taken the full two and one half minutes to die. Another girl danced *The Dying Swan.* I gave her arms a 9, but her legs got no better than a 4. The MC got a 5 from me when he introduced a piano medley by saying, "She will end with Mantovani's 'Love Story,' considered by many critics as the greatest love song of all time."

There was a twenty-minute break for the judges to select the five finalists. The woman in front of me talked some more about the singing priest and could you believe that plump girl up there in the bathing suit. The time passed quickly and soon people were back in their seats for Father Tom Smith's second number. This time he sang "I Want to Get Married." The lyrics were about women and what Father Tom would look for if the Pope in Rome would let him. After a series of hip thrusts he asked, "Anyway, who would want to marry an unwed father?" And so Father Tom Smith ended his second number to thunderous applause.

With a round of appropriate music from the organist, John Riley called off the names of the five finalists. They sat together on a row of chairs, and several held hands just the way they do at Atlantic City. Then the second runner-up, and the first runner-up were announced. Finally, after what seemed an interminably long time, John Riley said, "This year's Miss Central Pennsylvania is Mary Beth Derry."

The crowd erupted into two minutes of continuous applause. Last year's winner and this year's winner hugged. Mary Beth, flowers in her hand and a tiara on her head, began her slow walk down the runway, heading for the state competition and whatever might follow.

The pageant was followed by a big party open to the public. There were food, a loud local band, and lots of happy people. One of the happiest was Miss Congeniality, Arlene Dowd. Arlene was still full of enthusiasm about the interviews, the judges, her chaperone, and the other girls. "Gosh," she said, "it's all been really fabulous. I'll never forget it." Most of the other girls appeared to be enjoying themselves, not terribly crushed by their defeat. Only one girl seemed bitter. She smiled like the others, but after I promised not to quote her she confided in me that she thought the interview had been trite and uninspiring. She also felt that the girl who had won had no talent, and even less personality.

Mary Beth's parents were very proud and a little exhausted. "The last few weeks," her mother said, "have just been hectic; schedules to keep, errands to run, gowns to select, and hairdos to decide on. But now all the sacrifices, all the sleepless hours seem worth it."

The winner was surrounded by a few of the relatives and friends who had come to the pageant to cheer her on. This wasn't Mary Beth's first beauty contest. In the last couple of years she had been Bedford County Junior Miss and first runner-up to the Homecoming Queen of Penn State's Altoona campus. But she said that this was by far her biggest thrill.

I asked Mrs. Derry what kind of little girl Mary Beth had been. "You know," Mrs. Derry said, "Mary Beth never really was a little girl. I remember when she was five; we took a trip to Florida and when we arrived she turned to her father and said, 'Daddy, please don't tell anyone I'm five. Let's pretend I'm six.'"

Jean Walters, last year's winner, and her family also seemed pleased. Jean had no real complaints, except that the scholarship she had won wasn't as large as she had hoped.

"I really enjoyed the year," Jean said. "I guess I have grown a lot, become more mature, and gained a lot of self-confidence. I'll always be proud of having been Miss Central Pennsylvania."

The last person I talked to was Toni, the twenty-five-year-old opera-singing contestant. "Toni," I said, "I can't figure you out. What on earth ever made you decide to enter this competition?"

"Vanity, hope, I don't know. People at school kept telling me I ought to enter. I never thought of myself as a beauty contest type. But everyone said that with talent supposedly counting 50 per cent I had a real good chance of winning."

"Come on," I said, "I could have told you this morning you weren't going to win, no matter how talented you were. You're attractive, but not in a Miss America way, you know that."

"I know, I know," she said. "I was a fool to listen to people. I made a mistake, what more do you want me to say? People encouraged me and I let them talk me into it."

"But Toni, you knew about the swimsuit competition. How could you subject yourself to that?"

"Please," she said, "don't mention it. I was embarrassed, really humiliated. How do you think I felt walking down the runway in a swimsuit with my students in the audience? I could have died. I thought of turning around, but I knew I couldn't."

"So it's the swimsuit competition that has you so upset," I said.

"No, what gets me is I didn't even make the finals. I'm not conceited but I know I'm talented, more talented than any of the other girls. I ran because of my talent and I didn't even make the finals."

We were both silent and then Toni, smiling a bit, said, "You know, the other day we had a practice run-through of the crowning ceremony. Just by chance I was chosen to play the winner, and for a fleeting second I felt it had really happened, that I was the Queen. I felt beautiful and believed that someone like me could really win."

The smile had disappeared and Toni was close to tears. She said she wasn't going to cry, because I would pity her. But she did start crying, and we both sat there till she stopped. ■

MONTGOMERY, ALABAMA

Two men on Bailey Island, one with a rifle, the other with a pistol, were shooting at an offshore floating target. I stood by watching until one of them asked me to join them. In the next thirty minutes we shot a hundred rounds of ammunition.

Naturally we didn't shoot in silence. One thing that seemed to irk them was the increasing number of poorly informed, overly equipped hunters. There were, they said, too many men who knew nothing about guns wandering through the woods. "Yeah," laughed one, "like the people who buy guns at Sears and then need to ask the salesman where the trigger is."

When we finished I said, "You fellows have been so nice, I'll take your picture and send you a copy."

"Naw, you don't need to do that."

"I know, but I want to."

They shuffled around a bit and then asked how they should pose.

"I don't know," I said. "Any way that makes you feel comfortable." ■

BAILEY ISLAND, MAINE

MINNEAPOLIS, MINNESOTA

INAUGURAL BALL, MONTGOMERY, ALABAMA

PHILADELPHIA, PENNSYLVANIA

HEALTH CLUB, DALLAS, TEXAS

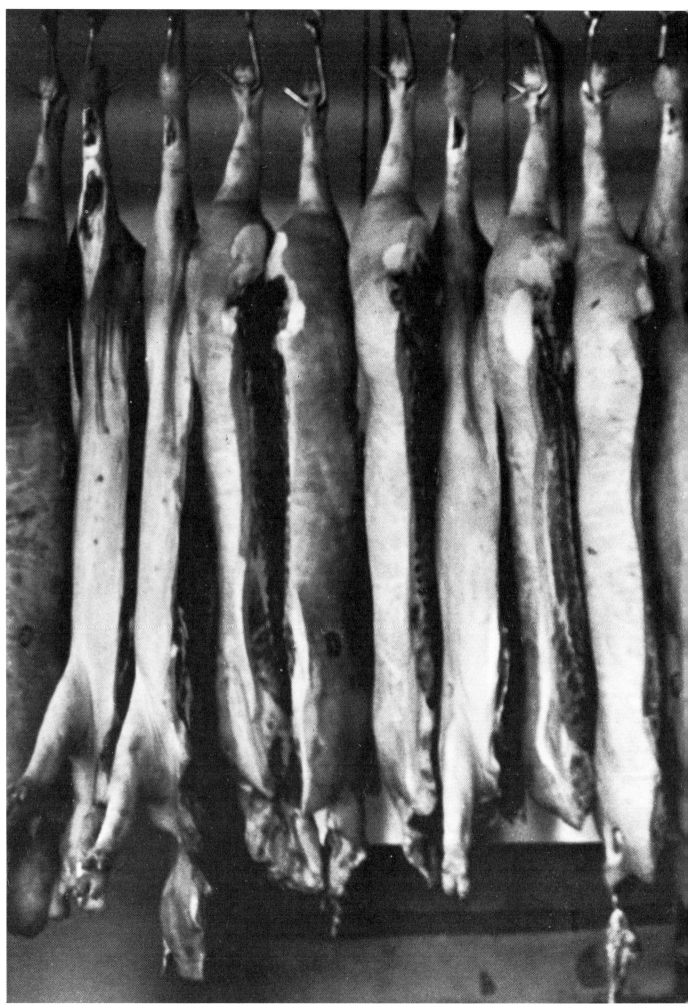

BOSTON, MASSACHUSETTS

BOSTON, MASSACHUSETTS

172

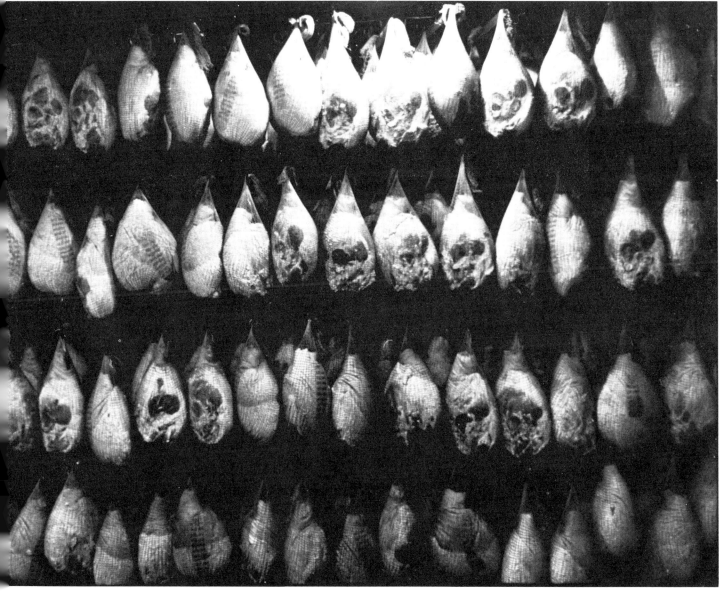

ANN ARBOR, MICHIGAN

DALLAS, TEXAS

ANN ARBOR, MICHIGAN

LLAMA, NEW MEXICO

DALLAS, TEXAS

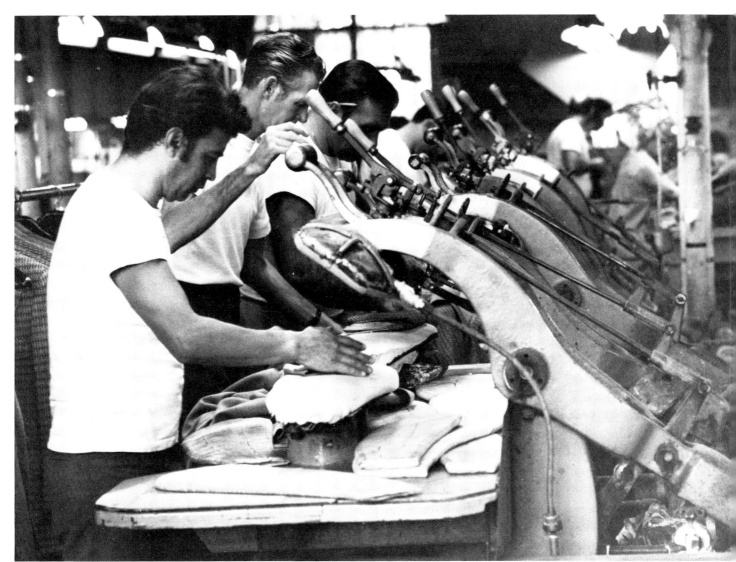

PHILADELPHIA, PENNSYLVANIA

178

Daroff's is located at 2300 Walnut Street, Philadelphia, Pennsylvania. Over eight hundred employees are engaged in the manufacture of suits in the block-long factory. Most of them take lunch between 12 and 1 P.M. The management staff and shop foremen take their lunch between 1 and 2 P.M.

At one o'clock, Harold Liptman, a shop foreman retiring after forty-seven years of service at Daroff's, was being honored with a luncheon at a nearby restaurant. Twenty-five men were invited to the luncheon at the company's expense. It was held in one of the restaurant's three oak-paneled rooms. There was no large table, so everyone was scattered around in several booths, each one holding four people. There was a head table saved for the guest of honor, Harold, the union representative, and the two Daroffs who direct the company's operation.

Conversation at my table turned almost immediately to whether or not a before-lunch drink was included in the luncheon. Someone said, "Sure, it must be included," and another person agreed that it ought to be, but no one ordered a drink until one of the Daroffs ordered his. "See, what did I tell you," the first man remarked.

Milt Levin, who had planned the luncheon and was sitting at my table, confided to us that people were already annoyed with him because they hadn't been invited to the luncheon and felt slighted. In defense of himself he said, "Look, I tried to keep it small and intimate, and kept it down to twenty-five people. Someone had to be left out; it isn't my fault."

Lunch arrived before people had finished their martinis, scotches, and gins. Milt had chosen halibut, though his first choice was filet of sole. He said he had been afraid that if he ordered filet of sole they might serve filet mignon by mistake, so lunch consisted of halibut, mashed potatoes, and peas.

While dessert and coffee were being served, the speeches began. Mike Daroff, one of the Daroff brothers who head the company, was the first to get up. He was a distinguished-looking man in a gray checked suit, with his hand wrapped around the remains of a Havana-Havana cigar. He looked at Harold and began.

"You know, Milt, I have known you for a long time, and you have been an important asset to the company's business. Yes, Milt, this business is like any team, you need a lot of good players to do well. We've been lucky with men like Mike, Tony, Joe and you. You have made a long and positive contribution to Daroff's and we'll miss you.

"I don't want you to think the relationship ends here with your retirement, Milt, I want you to know that whenever you need a suit you can still get it wholesale, plus the two dollars for handling." Everyone laughed, and Mike Daroff sat down.

He rose again, remembering that he was the MC, and began calling on other people. The first person he called on was the designer, who was wedged into a corner booth and tried unsuccessfully to stand up. In an awkward three-quarter standing position, his legs not quite emerging from under the table, he talked about Harold's work and their relationship over the years, as did Mike Daroff's brother Joe.

Then it was the union chief's turn to speak. He was a short, stocky man, well dressed in a gray pinstripe suit, holding a bowler hat in one hand and a White Owl cigar in the other. He said that he was nearly as old as Harold, but wasn't contemplating retiring soon. "No, I'm afraid the Daroffs will have to deal with me for several years. I believe that there is a healthy tension which exists between us. I know it is a tension I enjoy. But that is beside the point. What I really want to say is, Harold, you're a fine man and a damn good foreman. You're a good foreman because your loyalties remain with the company, and yet you're able to relate to the people in the shop. You're a man everyone associated with can be proud of.

"Oh, and Harold, I want you to know that any time you want a drink you come down to my office and I'll take you out and there won't be any service or handling charge." More laughter and the union chief sat down.

Now Harold himself was asked for a few comments. He stood up and his six foot two frame stretched far above the table. He appeared too young and vigorous to be retiring.

"Today," he began, "is a special day for me." Looking over at Mike and Joe Daroff he continued, "I appreciate what the Daroffs have done for me over the years, and this chance to have lunch with so many of my friends. You know, I came to work at Daroff's in 1924. When I came to the company I had a letter of reference and spoke to Mike and Joe's father about work. He looked at my reference, talked to me for a few minutes, and told me I could have a job, and that if I did well there would be steady employment for me. I suppose forty-seven years is steady enough.

"You know," he continued, "this may sound funny to some of you fellas, but my memories of my years here are fond ones. Sure there were bad times as well as good ones, and sure there were times when work was hard, but my mind somehow forgets the bad times and remembers the good ones. I look back over the years and have memories, fond memories of people I've worked with and the work that was done in my shop."

"Some people say to me, 'Harold, don't retire, you'll regret it.' They say that I'll be bored and that I'll miss the work which has been such a major part of my life. Well, I have other friends who aren't miserable in their retirement. In fact, some of them seem to be having a ball. Anyway, I've decided that I've worked long enough, and I'm looking forward to my retirement. As you know, my wife and I are going on a trip around the world, and when we come back I'll start thinking about what I want to do with all my free time. Again, I want to thank you all for this luncheon. It has been an honor to work at Daroff's."

Mike Daroff stood up again, and said, "You know, Harold, while you're on your trip we will all be busy working, and I hope you'll think of us." A stub of a cigar still in his hand, Mike continued, "We can't send you on a trip without some help, so we got you some luggage. Now, most people don't know it but there are two kinds of Dior luggage. There is Christian Dior, and there is Jewish Dior. We decided to get you some of the Christian Dior luggage." A lot of laughter.

While one of the pieces from the matched set was being unpacked, the men at my table began talking about retirement and the company's policy. One of the men said that Daroff's had instituted its own management pension plan which included foremen in 1934. Somehow Harold had not joined it and had stuck instead with the union pension plan. "It's a shame," said George. "If Harold had taken the company plan he could be retiring now with a pension between $40,000 and $50,000, which he could take either in one big chunk or over the years. But instead he's retiring under the union plan, and will only receive about $5,000."

Harold had finished inspecting the luggage, and held it high in the air for everyone else to see. The luncheon was over. We had entered the restaurant at about one-fifteen and were leaving less than an hour later. On the way out several men slapped Harold on the back, wishing him well. One man asked Harold if he could still get it up. ■   181

PHILADELPHIA, PENNSYLVANIA

NEW YORK CITY

NEW YORK CITY

NEW YORK CITY

185

NEW YORK CITY

NEW YORK CITY

FORT LAUDERDALE, FLORIDA

BETHLEHEM, PENNSYLVANIA

187

CAMBRIDGE, MASSACHUSETTS

GALLUP, NEW MEXICO

HOUSTON, TEXAS

CLEVELAND, OHIO

ELLENSBURG, WASHINGTON